Special thanks:

The photographer and publisher offer their sincere thanks to Hanimex (NZ) Limited the agents for Fuji Photo Film Company in New Zealand who have endorsed this book and through their support made possible a total New Zealand publication.
The majority of photographs printed within this publication were taken on Fujichrome transparency film.
The following descriptions highlight some of the advantages Fuji film offers under specific lighting conditions.

Fuji Velvia

Page 8. Pre-sunrise on Velvia. Holds subtle tones. Good vivid reproduction of colour without being garish.

Pages 15-16, 20, 32-33. A good vivid reproduction of the blues and greens while maintaining detail in the shadows and highlights.

Pages 18, 19. Velvia is ideal for autumn colour. Excellent reproduction of the autumn tones and good vivid greens.

Page 35. Velvia is a very good film for separating subtle tones and when properly exposed, will record a very wide range of shadow and highlight detail.

Pages 37, 58, 64, 74-75. These images are good examples of the magic of Fuji Velvia. Vivid greens and blues without degradation of the warm tones. This is a very fine grain and sharp film which in many cases has made the difference between an average photograph and a good photograph.

Fuji RDP 120 (now Provia 100)

Front Cover. At 100 ISO Fuji RDP was ideal for this situation. Early morning light, sheep, dogs, horses and people on the move. 100 ISO was fast enough to freeze the motion. Shadow and highlight detail is maintained and this film does not drift to excessively warm tones in sunrise or sunset situations.

Page 2-3. Accurate sunrise rendition with very good detail retention at the highlight extremes.

Pages 10, 28, 44. Shows again the well balanced contrast range of this film and shadow/highlight detail retention.

Pages 65, 70-71, 80-81. RDP ideal in higher contrast situations in forests. Good accurate colour rendition while holding detail in the brighter waterfall and sunlit foliage, while retaining good shadow detail.

Pages 52-53. Early morning, dramatic contrast range, a slowly moving boat in the middle distance and the camera platform a boat which is rolling slightly. The only solution was push RDP to 200 ISO. Colour rendition and contrast range is still excellent.

Pages 60, 62-63. Aerial photography in lowlight situations require that RDP be pushed 2 stops to 400 ISO. Any colour shift would have shown in the snow but colour rendition and contrast is still great.

Pages 76-77. A polarising filter in early morning light from a helicopter. RDP pushed one stop to 200 ISO. Good accurate colour and contrast.

Spectacular
NEW ZEALAND

Panoramic views of New Zealand

Thank You

The publishers offer their sincere thanks to the sponsors who have endorsed this book and through their kind support allowed Spectacular New Zealand to be produced as a totally New Zealand product.

COLORTRONIC IMAGES LTD CHRISTCHURCH - specialising in scanning, filmwork, electronic pre-press and plates to the graphic arts and printing industries are proud to be associated with the production of the Spectacular New Zealand book.

SPICER PAPER LIMITED "Committed to keeping printing in New Zealand". Auckland, Hamilton, Napier, Wellington, Christchurch and Dunedin.

RANGIORA PRINTING SERVICE Ph 0-3-313 7575 Fax 0-3-313 8803 Dedicated to producing top quality printing within New Zealand to help sustain ongoing employment and a buoyant economy.

F. CARTWRIGHT & SON LTD The South Island's largest Print Finishers. We pride ourselves in doing quality work with personal service for the Printing Industry in New Zealand. Ph 0-3-366 1764 Fax 0-3-366 6915.

Pirongia Range; & Waikato Farmland ▶

◀ Cape Reinga lighthouse located at the North Western extremity of New Zealand.

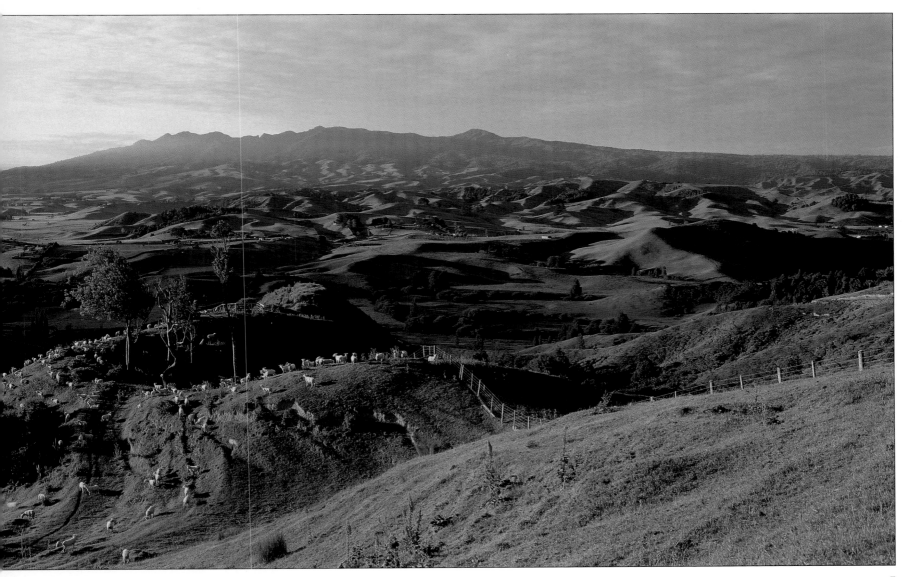

The Photographer

Andris Apse and his mother arrived in New Zealand when he was only six after several years spent in European refugee camps. Perhaps these early miseries contributed to Andris's later dislike of cities and his love for the openness of coast and wilderness. Growing up mainly in rural New Zealand, he started working on farms at 16 and later joined the Forest Service. Their projects carried him far from the gentleness of the Bay of Islands and rolling farmland of the North Island, into the back country of the Southern Alps and Fiordland. Quickly captivated by the grandeur of these remote reaches, he purchased a basic camera and started taking snaps. In 1970 he took the opportunity to purchase a small photographic business in Rangiora, north of Christchurch. To be sure, he was now a professional photographer, but as with many, the early years were spent in weddings, portraiture, and commercial photography—not what really excited him.

The year he broke out was 1978, when he spent a vast sum on a Linhof Technorama camera—one of only a few in the country— that could take 6 cm by 17 cm transparencies—an image size commensurate with the magnificence of his wild panoramas! In the early 1980s, accompanied by his wife and three youngish children, Andris spent a year roaming 45000 km through the byways of Chile, seeking to capture powerful images of landscapes. It proved to be one of the most rewarding and enjoyable years of his career. No commercial constraints, just aesthetics. After Chile, he devoted himself largely to landscape photography, and in the decade and more since that decision, Andris has had commissioned assignments in Hawaii, Japan, Singapore, Canada, Tahiti, Britain, Australia, Thailand, the USA, and of course New Zealand. Within New Zealand he has travelled everywhere, returning to potentially photogenic spots time and again, with the patience necessary to capture the quintessential moods of the land and elements on film. Of all the places Andris has visited, Fiordland still draws him the most strongly, and he would be content to confine his photography to its remote and harsh wonders. Like many great photographer's images, Andris's photographs of the land possess the curious magnetism of inspiring in the beholders a strong desire to experience the area for themselves. His sublime, fascinating images have appeared in books and periodicals all over the world, and his talents, effort, and skill have been recognised by numerous international photographic awards. These include winning the Animal Behaviour section of the 1984 British Museum Wildlife Photographer of the Year competition (13000 entries), winner of the Olympus Seventieth Anniversary International Photographic Competition in Japan (in 1990, a contest with 24000 entries), and securing Gold Awards in the Hong Kong-based Pacific Asia Travel Association, Travel Photograph category in 1992 and Travel Poster category in 1994.

Andris making camp on the Auckland Islands

Introduction

New Zealand. A sparsely peopled slither, stretching from the sub-tropics to the sub-antarctic, deep ocean for thousands of kilometers in every direction. A spinnaker stretched out across the wind, churned by earthquakes, scarred by volcanic boils—some steaming still, drenched by rain. Adrift from other land masses for tens of millions of years bearing a cargo of relic plants and discontinued animals. With temperate forests dense as tropic jungle, mountains fierce and high, rocky river beds kilometres across, beaches and dunes, deserted, stretching beyond the curve of the world. And yet sparkling bays with scurrying yachts, still sounds and mirror lakes, green farms with deer, kiwifruit, lamb, wheat, and vine. Glaciers plunging past parrots towards the surf. Clear skies dense with stars. New Zealand, modest in size, rich in wonders.

"This curious world which we inhabit is more wonderful than it is convenient; more beautiful than it is useful . . . more to be admired and enjoyed than used." (Thoreau).

◀ Dramatic sunrise on Kaikoura's rocky coast

▼ Sperm whale sounding at Kaikoura - Marlborough

Surfcasting the clear blue waters - Opononi, Northland

New Zealanders favourite pastime, picking pipis on Taipa Bay
beach, Northland

▲ Native kauri trees Coromandel Peninsula

◀ Cascading Waihi Falls - Hawkes Bay

Overleaf:
Southern Alps reflections - Ahuriri Valley, Otago

17

Quaint historical cottages line Arrowtown's narrow streets

Autumn splendour at Macetown central Otago with snow
capped mountains as a backdrop

Coastal native forest reflected in Okarito Lagoon - Westland,
with Mount Cook and the Southern Alps as a backdrop

White Herons at nest on the banks of the Waitangiroto river - Westland

Overleaf:

The Ben Ohou Range as viewed from Lake Pukaki

Crystal clear waters explore the bays of Moturau Island in the ▶
Bay of Islands

Paihia beach - Bay of Islands, Northland ▼

Rolling green pastures in the central North Island near Turangi

Koroniti Marae located along the historical Whanganui river

The tranquility of Fiordland National Park is reflected in this view of the
Hall Arm at Doubtful Sound

This aerial view of the Marlborough Sounds encompasses both the
Tory Channel and Queen Charlotte Sound on the right.

▲ Natures forest ferny floor - King Country

◀ Pukakaunui waterfall on the Cathins river - Southland

Overleaf: Salmond fishing on the Rakaia river

Mount Ngauruhoe 2,290m situated in the Tongariro National Park

White Island - New Zealand's most active volcano

Sunset on Lake Wanaka - Central Otago

Vineyard situated on the shoreline of Lake Hayes

▲ Crimson Pohutukawa tree in flower

◄ Native bush & crystal waters in Fiordland
National Park

Overleaf: The Southern Alps reflected in Lake Matheson

▲ Late evening sailing on the sparkling Waitamata Harbour

◄ Rangitoto Islands volcanic cone is located at the entrance to the Waitemata Harbour, gateway to Auckland City

Otago Peninsula from Peggy's Hill

The incredible Moeraki Boulders - Otago

Lake Wakatipu and Queenstown as viewed from the Remarkable's ski field

The mighty Kawerau River near Queenstown is popular for jet boating,
waterskiing and fishing

Fly fishing at sunset - Lake Moana, Westland

▲ The Sutherland Falls tumble 580m to Milford Sound

◄ Spring lambs feed on new pasture at Fairlie, South Canterbury

Overleaf: Mitre Peak 1695m emerging from cloud at Milford Sound, Fiordland National Park

Overleaf: Reflections of the Southern Alps near Fox Glacier, Westland.

Sunset over Dusky Sound, Fiordland National Park ▶

Castle point on the Wairarapa Coast ▼

Lush green farmland in the King Country, Central North Island

Blenheim vineyards - Located in the Marlborough district

Mount Aspiring and the Bonar Glacier - Mount Aspiring National Park

Incredible views of Queenstown, Lake Wakatipu and the
Remarkable Mountains

Overleaf: Franz Josef Glacier - Westland National Park

Mount Cook viewed from Lake Pukaki through autumn splendour

Native bush - Te Urewera National Park

Tanemahuta - New Zealand's largest Kauri tree located in the
Waipua forest, Northland

Cartwheels of hay with Mount Taranaki as a backdrop

Overleaf: Huka Falls - These extensive falls at the head of the Waikato river, flow from Lake Taupo to form New Zealands longest river

◄ The spectacular Korokoro Falls on the Te Korokorowhaitiri stream near Lake Waikaremoana within the Te Urewera National Park

▼ Motu river mouth - East cape, Bay of Plenty

Northern Royal Albatross and chick - Tairaroa Head, Otago

Tasman mountains viewed from Mount Owen, Nelson

The violent eruption of Mount Ruapehu contrasts with
the tranquil farm setting in the foreground.

Balloon Safaris over the Canterbury Plains with a snow covered Mount Hutt range as a backdrop.

Pancake Rocks, Punakaiki National Park - Westland

Ice climbing on the Fox Glacier - Westland

Overleaf: Located at Waikaremoana in the North Islands Te Urewera National Park. This beautiful native bush and forest is easily accessable by the many walks through the park.

▲ The Champagne pool with its bubbling hot water and colourful surrounds is the main attraction at the Waitapu thermal area south of Rotorua

◀ Pohutu Geyser sends scalding water high into the sky to provide a world renowned display at Whakarewarewa Thermal reserve Rotorua

Spectacular New Zealand

ISBN 0-908973-07-1

Photographs by: Andris Apse
Text by: Warren Judd

First published in 1995 by
First Class Publications Ltd.
PO Box 6936, Wellesley Street, Auckland, New Zealand.
Phone: 0-9-570 1000, Fax: 0-9-570 1010.

Printed by Rangiora Print, Rangiora.
Designed by Martin Lovatt of Glenn Conroy Creative.

Many of the images in this book are available as Limited Edition
Photographic Prints.
For further information, contact: First Class Publications Ltd.